Traditional Carols

kevin mayhew

The Dorset Music House
Sherborne
01935 816332

Acknowledgements

The publishers wish to express their gratitude to the copyright holders who have granted permission to include their material in this book.

Every effort has been made to trace the copyright holders of all the songs in this collection and we hope that no copyright has been infringed. Apology is made and pardon sought if the contrary be the case, and a correction will be made in any reprint of this book.

Important Copyright Information

We would like to remind users of this carol book that the reproduction of any song texts or music without the permission of the copyright holder is illegal. Details of all copyright holders are clearly indicated below each song.

Many of the song *texts* may be covered either by a Christian Copyright Licensing (CCL) licence or a Calamus licence. If you possess a CCL or Calamus licence, it is essential that you check your instruction manual to ensure that the song you wish to use is covered.

If you are *not* a member of CCL or Calamus, or the song you wish to reproduce is not covered by your licence, you must contact the copyright holder direct for their permission.

Christian Copyright Licensing (Europe) Ltd. have also now introduced a *Music Reproduction Licence*. Again, if you hold such a licence it is essential that you check your instruction manual to ensure that the song you wish to reproduce is covered. The reproduction of any music not covered by your licence is both illegal and immoral.

If you are interested in joining CCL or Calamus they can be contacted at the following addresses:

Christian Copyright Licensing (Europe) Ltd., P.O. Box 1339, Eastbourne,
East Sussex, BN21 1AD.
Tel: 01323 417711, Fax: 01323 417722.

Calamus, 30 North Terrace, Mildenhall, Suffolk, IP28 7AB.
Tel: 01638 716579, Fax: 01638 510390.

We hope you enjoy *Traditional Carols*. Further copies are available from your local stockist.
In case of difficulty, or to request a catalogue, please contact the publisher direct by writing to:
The Sales Department, KEVIN MAYHEW LTD, Buxhall, Stowmarket, Suffolk IP14 3BW
Phone 01449 737978   Fax 01449 737834   E-mail info@kevinmayhewltd.com

---

First published in Great Britain in 2004 by Kevin Mayhew Ltd.

© Copyright 2004 Kevin Mayhew Ltd.

ISBN 1 84417 260 0
ISMN M 57024 346 4
Catalogue No: 1450323

0 1 2 3 4 5 6 7 8 9

Cover design by Jo Balaam
Printed and bound in Great Britain

Contents

Page No

1	A great and mighty wonder	5
2	Angels from the realms of glory	6
3	Away in a manger	8
4	Child in the manger	11
5	Christians, awake!	12
6	Ding dong, merrily on high!	15
7	God rest you merry, gentlefolk	16
8	Good Christians all, rejoice	18
9	Good King Wenceslas	20
10	Go, tell it on the mountain	23
11	Hark, the herald-angels sing	24
12	Infant holy, infant lowly	27
13	In the bleak mid-winter	28
14	It came upon the midnight clear	30
15	Joy to the world!	32
16	Little Jesus, sweetly sleep	33
17	Love came down at Christmas	34
18	Mary had a baby	35
19	O come, all ye faithful	36
20	Of the Father's love begotten	38
21	O little one sweet, O little one mild	40
22	O little town of Bethlehem	42
23	Once in royal David's city	45
24	On Christmas night all Christians sing	46
25	See, amid the winter's snow	48
26	Silent night	51
27	The angel Gabriel from heaven came	52
28	The first Nowell	54
29	The holly and the ivy	57
30	There's a star in the East	58
31	The Virgin Mary had a baby boy	60
32	Unto us a boy is born	63
33	We three kings of Orient are	64
34	What child is this	66
35	While shepherds watched	67

Traditional Carols

1 A great and mighty wonder

St Germanus (c.634-c.734) trans.
John Mason Neale (1818-1866)

German carol melody, harmonies based
on Michael Praetorius (1571-1621) alt.

ES IST EIN' ROS' ENTSPRUNGEN 76 76 676

1. A great and mighty wonder, a full and holy cure! The Virgin bears the infant with virgin honour pure:

Refrain
Repeat the hymn again! 'To God on high be glory, and peace on earth shall reign.'

2. The Word becomes incarnate,
and yet remains on high;
and cherubim sing anthems
to shepherds from the sky:

3. While thus they sing your monarch,
those bright angelic bands,
rejoice, ye vales and mountains,
ye oceans, clap your hands:

4. Since all he comes to ransom
by all be he adored,
the infant born in Bethl'em,
the Saviour and the Lord:

2 Angels from the realms of glory

James Montgomery (1771-1854)

French or Flemish melody
arr. Charles Wood (1866-1926)

IRIS 87 87 and Refrain

1. An-gels from the realms of glo-ry, wing your flight o'er all the earth; ye who sang cre-a-tion's sto-ry now pro-claim Mes-si-ah's birth: *Refrain* Come and wor-ship

2. Shepherds, in the field abiding,
   watching o'er your flocks by night,
   God with us is now residing,
   yonder shines the infant Light:

3. Sages, leave your contemplations;
   brighter visions beam afar;
   seek the great Desire of Nations;
   ye have seen his natal star:

4. Saints before the altar bending,
   watching long in hope and fear,
   suddenly the Lord, descending,
   in his temple shall appear:

5. Though an infant now we view him,
   he shall fill his Father's throne,
   gather all the nations to him;
   ev'ry knee shall then bow down:

3 Away in a manger

William James Kirkpatrick
Alternative vs. 2&3: Michael Forster (b.1946)

William James Kirkpatrick (1838-1921)
arr. Colin Mawby

CRADLE SONG 11 11 11 11

1. A-way in a man-ger, no crib for a bed, the lit-tle Lord Je-sus laid down his sweet head. The stars in the bright sky looked down where he lay, the lit-tle Lord Je-sus a-sleep on the hay.

Alternative version of vs. 2&3 © Copyright 1996 Kevin Mayhew Ltd.
This arrangement © Copyright 2004 Kevin Mayhew Ltd.

2. The cattle are lowing, the baby awakes,
   but little Lord Jesus, no crying he makes.
   I love thee, Lord Jesus! Look down from the sky,
   and stay by my side until morning is nigh.

3. Be near me, Lord Jesus; I ask thee to stay
   close by me for ever, and love me, I pray.
   Bless all the dear children in thy tender care,
   and fit us for heaven, to live with thee there.

Alternative text for verses 2 and 3:

2. The cattle are lowing, they also adore
   the little Lord Jesus who lies in the straw.
   I love you, Lord Jesus, I know you are near
   to love and protect me till morning is here.

3. Be near me, Lord Jesus; I ask you to stay
   close by me for ever, and love me, I pray.
   Bless all the dear children in your tender care,
   prepare us for heaven, to live with you there.

William James Kirkpatrick (1838-1921)
arr. Richard Lloyd

A unison arrangement

1. A-way in a man-ger, no crib for a bed, the lit-tle Lord Je-sus laid down his sweet head. The stars in the bright sky looked down where he lay, the lit-tle Lord Je-sus a-sleep on the hay.

This arrangement © Copyright 1996 Kevin Mayhew Ltd.

Traditional
Carols

4 Child in the manger

Mary MacDonald (1817-1890)
trans. Lachlan MacBean (1853-1931)

Traditional Gaelic melody
arr. Colin Mawby

BUNESSAN 55 54 D
Unison

1. Child in the manger, infant of Mary;
outcast and stranger, Lord of all;
child who inherits all our transgressions,
all our demerits on him fall.

2. Once the most holy child of salvation
gently and lowly lived below;
now as our glorious mighty Redeemer,
see him victorious o'er each foe.

3. Prophets foretold him, infant of wonder;
angels behold him on his throne;
worthy our Saviour of all their praises;
happy for ever are his own.

This arrangement © Copyright 2004 Kevin Mayhew Ltd.

5 Christians, awake!

John Byrom (1692-1763) alt. John Wainwright (1723-1768)

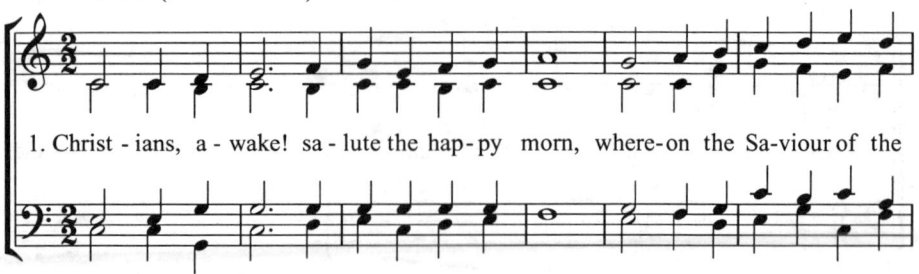

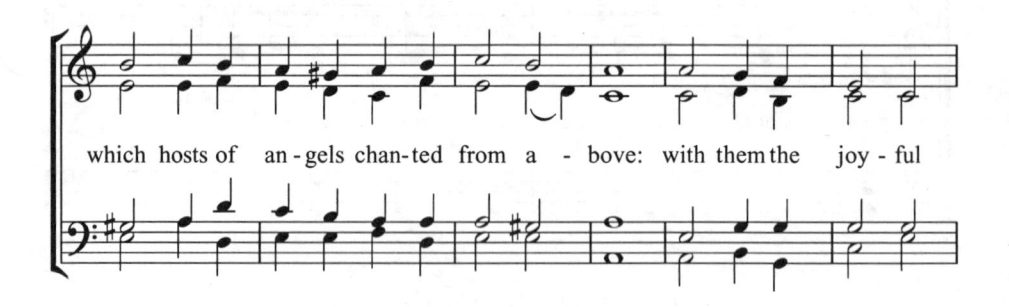

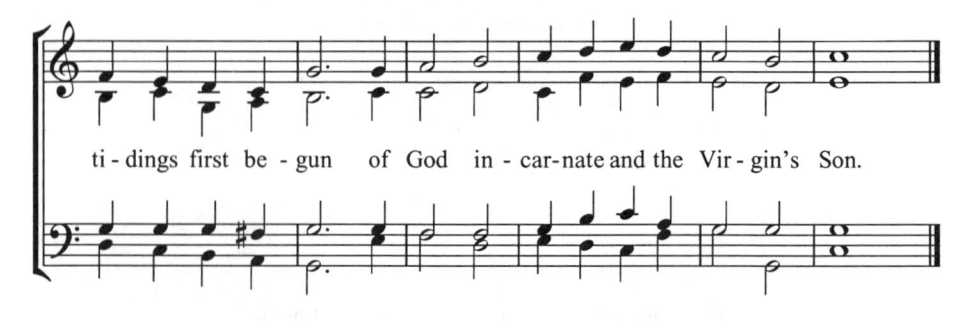

YORKSHIRE (STOCKPORT) 10 10 10 10 10 10

1. Christians, awake! salute the happy morn, whereon the Saviour of the world was born; rise to adore the mystery of love, which hosts of angels chanted from above: with them the joyful tidings first begun of God incarnate and the Virgin's Son.

2. Then to the watchful shepherds it was told,
   who heard th'angelic herald's voice, 'Behold,
   I bring good tidings of a Saviour's birth
   to you and all the nations on the earth:
   this day hath God fulfilled his promised word,
   this day is born a Saviour, Christ the Lord.'

3. He spake; and straightway the celestial choir
   in hymns of joy, unknown before, conspire;
   the praises of redeeming love they sang,
   and heav'n's whole orb with alleluias rang:
   God's highest glory was their anthem still,
   peace on the earth, in ev'ry heart good will.

4. To Bethl'em straight th'enlightened shepherds ran,
   to see, unfolding, God's eternal plan,
   and found, with Joseph and the blessèd maid,
   her Son, the Saviour, in a manger laid:
   then to their flocks, still praising God, return,
   and their glad hearts with holy rapture burn.

5. O may we keep and ponder in our mind
   God's wondrous love in saving lost mankind;
   trace we the babe, who hath retrieved our loss,
   from his poor manger to his bitter cross;
   tread in his steps, assisted by his grace,
   till our first heav'nly state again takes place.

6. Then may we hope, th'angelic hosts among,
   to sing, redeemed, a glad triumphal song:
   he that was born upon this joyful day
   around us all his glory shall display;
   saved by his love, incessant we shall sing
   eternal praise to heav'n's almighty King.

Traditional Carols

6 Ding dong, merrily on high!

George Ratcliffe Woodward (1848-1934)

Traditional French melody
arr. Charles Wood (1866-1926)

BRANSLE DE L'OFFICIAL 77 77 and Refrain

1. Ding dong, merrily on high! In heav'n the bells are ringing; ding dong, verily the sky is riv'n with angel singing.

Refrain
Gloria, hosanna in excelsis!

2. E'en so here below, below,
   let steeple bells be swungen,
   and io, io, io,
   by priest and people sungen.

3. Pray you, dutifully prime
   your matin chime, ye ringers;
   may you beautifully rhyme
   your evetime song, ye singers.

Text © Copyright SPCK, Holy Trinity Church, Marylebone Road, London NW1 4DU.

7 God rest you merry, gentlefolk

Traditional English alt.

Traditional English melody
arr. John Stainer (1840-1901)

GOD REST YOU MERRY 86 86 86 and Refrain

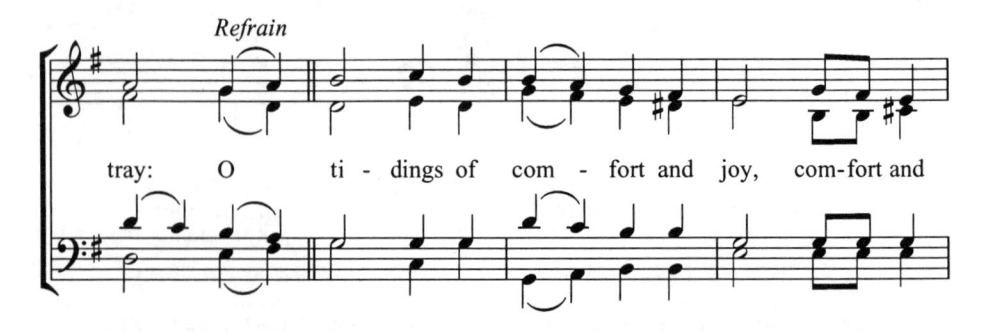

1. God rest you mer-ry, gen-tle-folk, let no-thing you dis-may, for Je-sus Christ our Sa-viour was born on Christ-mas Day, to save us all from Sa-tan's pow'r when we were gone as-tray: *Refrain* O ti-dings of com-fort and joy, com-fort and

joy, O ti - dings of com - fort and joy.

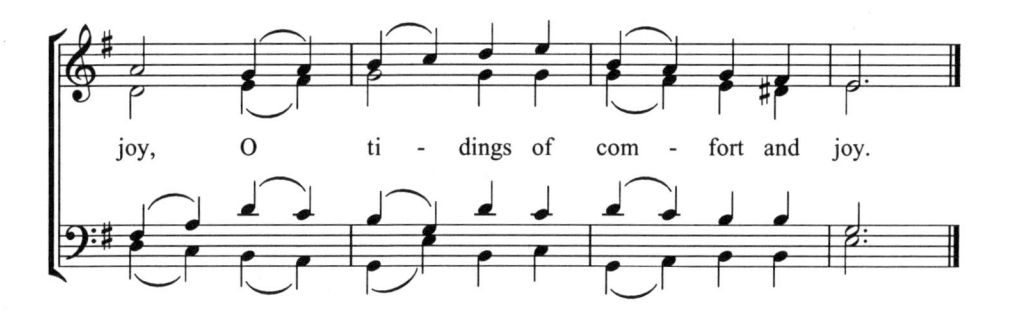

2. In Bethlehem, in Jewry,
this blessèd babe was born,
and laid within a manger,
upon this blessèd morn;
at which his mother Mary
did nothing take in scorn:

3. From God, our heav'nly Father,
a blessèd angel came,
and unto certain shepherds,
brought tidings of the same,
how that in Bethlehem was born
the Son of God by name:

4. 'Fear not,' then said the angel,
'let nothing you affright,
this day is born a Saviour,
of virtue, pow'r and might;
by him the world is overcome
and Satan put to flight.'

5. The shepherds at those tidings,
rejoicèd much in mind,
and left their flocks a-feeding,
in tempest, storm and wind,
and went to Bethlehem straightway,
this blessèd babe to find:

6. But when to Bethlehem they came,
whereat this infant lay,
they found him in a manger,
where oxen feed on hay;
his mother Mary kneeling,
unto the Lord did pray:

7. Now to the Lord sing praises,
all you within this place,
and with true love and fellowship
each other now embrace;
this holy tide of Christmas
all others doth deface:

8 Good Christians all, rejoice

John Mason Neale (1818-1866) alt.

14th century German carol melody
arr. John Stainer

IN DULCI JUBILO 66 79 78 55

1. Good Christians all, rejoice with heart and soul and voice! Give ye heed to what we say: News! News! Jesus Christ is born to-day; ox and ass before him bow, and he is in the manger now:

Christ is born to - day, Christ is born to - day!

2. Good Christians all, rejoice
   with heart and soul and voice!
   Now ye hear of endless bliss:
   Joy! Joy! Jesus Christ was born for this.
   He hath opened heaven's door,
   and we are blest for evermore:
   Christ was born for this,
   Christ was born for this.

3. Good Christians all, rejoice
   with heart and soul and voice!
   Now ye need not fear the grave:
   Peace! Peace! Jesus Christ was born to save;
   calls you one, and calls you all,
   to gain his everlasting hall:
   Christ was born to save,
   Christ was born to save.

9 Good King Wenceslas

John Mason Neale (1818-1866) alt.

Piae Cantiones (1582)
arr. John Stainer

TEMPUS ADEST FLORIDUM 76 76 D

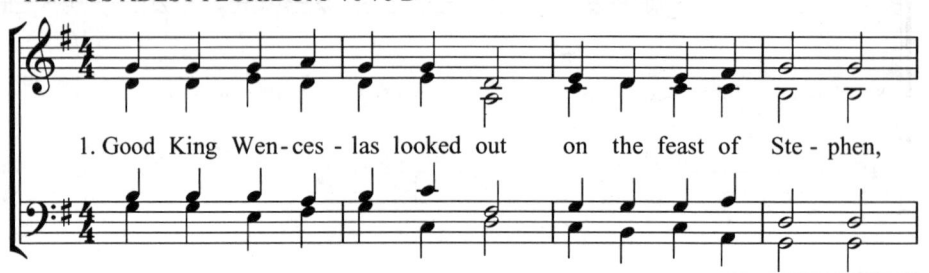

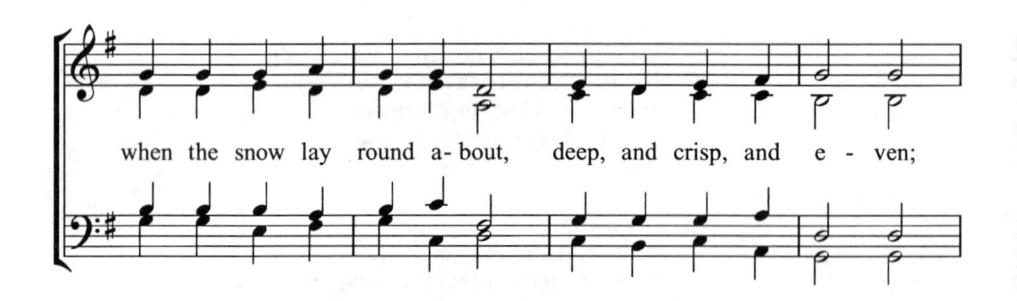

1. Good King Wenceslas looked out on the feast of Stephen,
when the snow lay round about, deep, and crisp, and even;
brightly shone the moon that night, though the frost was cruel,
when a poor man came in sight, gath-'ring winter fuel.

2. 'Hither, page, and stand by me,
   if thou know'st it, telling,
   yonder peasant, who is he,
   where and what his dwelling?'
   'Sire, he lives a good league hence,
   underneath the mountain,
   right against the forest fence,
   by Saint Agnes' fountain.'

3. 'Bring me flesh, and bring me wine,
   bring me pine logs hither:
   thou and I will see him dine,
   when we bring him thither.'
   Page and monarch, forth they went,
   forth they went together;
   through the rude wind's wild lament,
   and the bitter weather.

4. 'Sire, the night is darker now,
   and the wind blows stronger;
   fails my heart, I know not how;
   I can go no longer.'
   'Mark my footsteps good, my page;
   tread thou in them boldly:
   thou shalt find the winter's rage
   freeze thy blood less coldly.'

5. In his master's steps he trod,
   where the snow lay dinted;
   heat was in the very sod
   which the Saint had printed.
   Therefore, Christians all, be sure,
   wealth or rank possessing,
   ye who now will bless the poor,
   shall yourselves find blessing.

Traditional
Carols

10 Go, tell it on the mountain

Traditional

Traditional
arr. Richard Lewis

Refrain
Unison

Go, tell it on the moun-tain, o-ver the hills and ev-'ry-where.

Go, tell it on the moun - tain that Je-sus Christ is born. 1. While

Last time

born. shep-herds kept their watch-ing o'er wand-'ring flocks by

night, be-hold, from out of heav-en, there shone a ho-ly light. *D.C.*

2. And lo, when they had seen it,
they all bowed down and prayed;
they travelled on together
to where the babe was laid.

3. When I was a seeker,
I sought both night and day:
I asked my Lord to help me
and he showed me the way.

4. He made me a watchman
upon the city wall,
and, if I am a Christian,
I am the least of all.

This arrangement © Copyright 2004 Kevin Mayhew Ltd.

11 Hark, the herald-angels sing

Charles Wesley (1707-1788),
George Whitefield (1714-1770),
Martin Madan (1726-1790)
and others, alt.

Adapted from Felix Mendelssohn (1809-1847)
by William Hayman Cummings (1831-1915)

MENDELSSOHN 77 77 D and Refrain

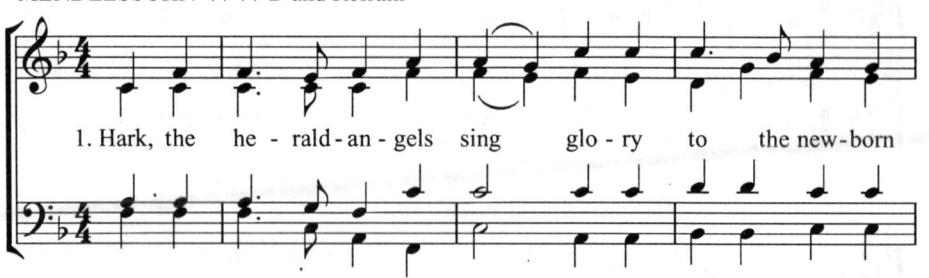

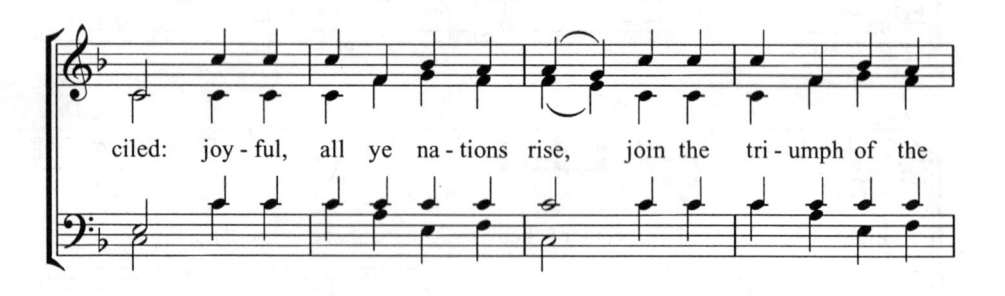

1. Hark, the he-rald-an-gels sing glo-ry to the new-born King; peace on earth and mer-cy mild, God and sin-ners re-con-ciled: joy-ful, all ye na-tions rise, join the tri-umph of the skies, with th'an-ge-lic host pro-claim, 'Christ is born in Beth-le-hem.'

Refrain   *Unison*

Hark, the he-rald-an-gels sing glo-ry to the new-born King.

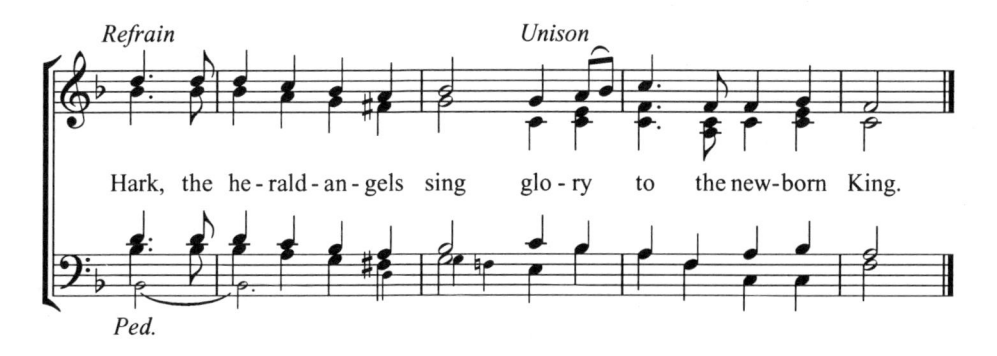

Ped.

2. Christ, by highest heav'n adored,
   Christ, the everlasting Lord,
   late in time behold him come,
   offspring of a virgin's womb!
   Veiled in flesh the Godhead see,
   hail, th'incarnate Deity!
   Pleased as man with us to dwell,
   Jesus, our Emmanuel.

3. Hail, the heav'n-born Prince of Peace!
   Hail, the Sun of Righteousness!
   Light and life to all he brings,
   ris'n with healing in his wings;
   mild he lays his glory by,
   born that we no more may die,
   born to raise us from the earth,
   born to give us second birth.

Traditional Carols

12 Infant holy, infant lowly

Traditional Polish
trans. Edith Margaret Gellibrand Reed (1885-1933)

Traditional Polish melody
arr. Colin Mawby

WZLOBIE LEZY 87 87 88 77

1. Infant holy, infant lowly, for his bed a cattle stall; oxen lowing, little knowing Christ the babe is Lord of all. Swift are winging angels singing, no-wells ringing, tidings bringing, Christ the babe is Lord of all, Christ the babe is Lord of all.

2. Flocks were sleeping, shepherds keeping
    vigil till the morning new;
    saw the glory, heard the story,
    tidings of a gospel true.
    Thus rejoicing, free from sorrow,
    praises voicing, greet the morrow,
    Christ the babe was born for you,
    Christ the babe was born for you.

This arrangement © Copyright 2004 Kevin Mayhew Ltd.

13 In the bleak mid-winter

Christina Georgina Rossetti (1830-1894) Gustav Holst (1874-1934)

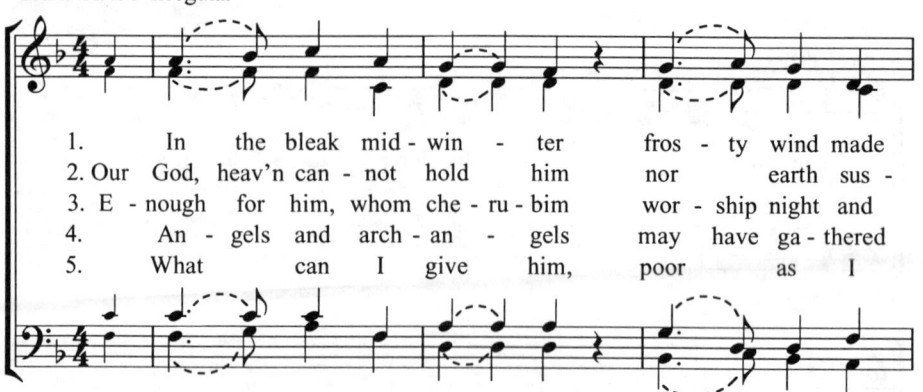

CRANHAM Irregular

1. In the bleak mid-winter frosty wind made moan, earth stood hard as iron, water like a stone; snow had fallen, snow on snow, snow on snow, in the bleak mid-winter, long ago.

2. Our God, heav'n cannot hold him nor earth sustain; heav'n and earth shall flee away when he comes to reign. In the bleak mid-winter a stable-place sufficed the Lord God Almighty, Jesus Christ.

3. Enough for him, whom cherubim worship night and day, a breastful of milk, and a mangerful of hay: enough for him, whom angels fall down before, the ox and ass and camel which adore.

4. Angels and archangels may have gathered there, cherubim and seraphim thronged the air; but only his mother, in her maiden bliss, worshipped the Beloved with a kiss.

5. What can I give him, poor as I am? If I were a shepherd I would bring a lamb; if I were a wise man I would do my part; yet what I can I give him — give my heart.

Music © Copyright Oxford University Press, Great Clarendon St., Oxford OX2 6DP.
Reproduced by permission from *The English Hymnal*.

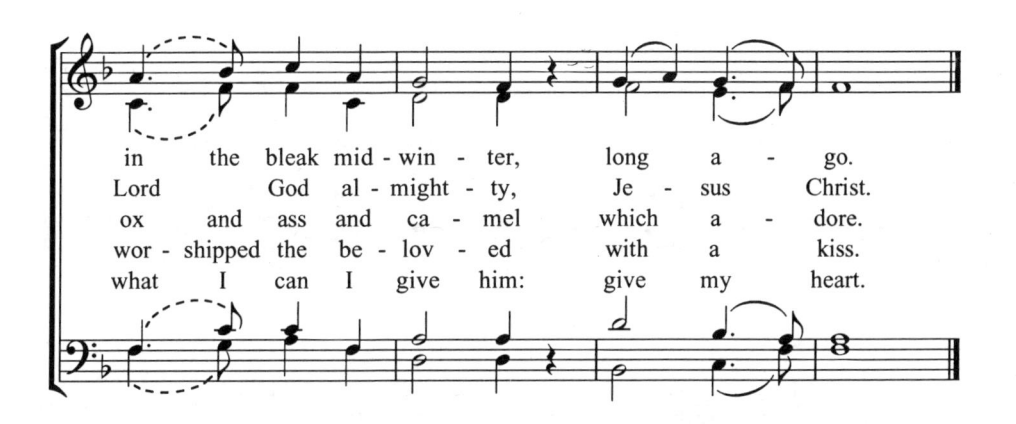

snow on snow, snow on snow,
win - ter a sta - ble - place suf - ficed the
an - gels fall down be - fore, the
mo - ther in her mai - den bliss
wise man I would do my part, yet

in the bleak mid - win - ter, long a - go.
Lord God al - might - ty, Je - sus Christ.
ox and ass and ca - mel which a - dore.
wor - shipped the be - lov - ed with a kiss.
what I can I give him: give my heart.

14 It came upon the midnight clear

Edmund Hamilton Sears (1810-1876) alt.

Traditional English melody
arr. Arthur Seymour Sullivan

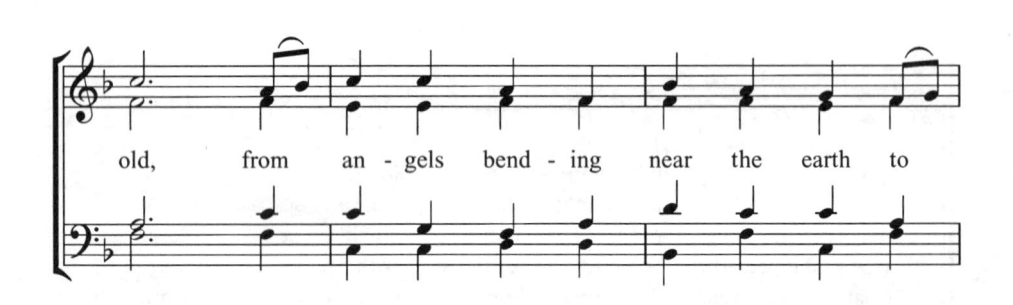

NOEL DCM

1. It came upon the midnight clear, that glorious song of old, from angels bending near the earth to touch their harps of gold: 'Peace on the earth, good-will to all, from heav'n's all-gracious King!' The world in solemn

still - ness lay to hear the an - gels sing.

2. Still through the cloven skies they come,
   with peaceful wings unfurled;
   and still their heav'nly music floats
   o'er all the weary world:
   above its sad and lowly plains
   they bend on hov'ring wing;
   and ever o'er its Babel-sounds
   the blessèd angels sing.

3. Yet with the woes of sin and strife
   the world has suffered long;
   beneath the angel-strain have rolled
   two thousand years of wrong;
   and warring humankind hears not
   the love-song which they bring;
   O hush the noise of mortal strife,
   and hear the angels sing!

4. And ye, beneath life's crushing load,
   whose forms are bending low,
   who toil along the climbing way
   with painful steps and slow:
   look now! for glad and golden hours
   come swiftly on the wing;
   O rest beside the weary road,
   and hear the angels sing.

5. For lo, the days are hast'ning on,
   by prophets seen of old,
   when with the ever-circling years
   comes round the age of gold;
   when peace shall over all the earth
   its ancient splendours fling,
   and all the world give back the song
   which now the angels sing.

15 Joy to the world!

Isaac Watts (1674-1748)
based on Psalm 98 alt.

George Frideric Handel (1685-1759)

ANTIOCH CM

1. Joy to the world! The Lord is come; let earth receive her King; let ev-'ry heart prepare him room, and heav'n and nature sing, and heav'n and nature sing, and heav'n, and heav'n and nature sing.

2. Joy to the earth! The Saviour reigns;
   let us our songs employ;
   while fields and floods, rocks, hills and plains
   repeat the sounding joy,
   repeat the sounding joy,
   repeat, repeat the sounding joy.

3. He rules the world with truth and grace,
   and makes the nations prove
   the glories of his righteousness,
   and wonders of his love,
   and wonders of his love,
   and wonders, and wonders of his love.

16 Little Jesus, sweetly sleep

Traditional Czech carol
trans. Percy Dearmer (1867-1936)
Alternative words: Christopher Massey (b.1956)

Traditional Czech carol
arr. Martin Shaw (1875-1958)

ROCKING 10 7 88 77

1. Lit-tle Je-sus, sweet-ly sleep, do not stir; we will lend a coat of fur;
2. Ma-ry's lit-tle ba-by sleep, sweet-ly sleep, sleep in com-fort, slum-ber deep;

we will rock you, rock you, rock you, we will rock you, rock you, rock you;
we will rock you, rock you, rock you, we will rock you, rock you, rock you;

see the fur to keep you warm, snug-ly round your ti-ny form.
we will serve you all we can, dar-ling, dar-ling lit-tle man.

Alternative words:

1. Little Jesus, sleep away, in the hay,
   while we worship, watch and pray.
   We will gather at the manger,
   worship this amazing stranger:
   little Jesus born on earth,
   sign of grace and human worth.

2. Little Jesus, sleep away, while you may;
   pain is for another day.
   While you sleep, we will not wake you,
   when you cry we'll not forsake you.
   Little Jesus, sleep away,
   we will worship you today.

Text and Music © Copyright Oxford University Press, Great Clarendon St., Oxford OX2 6DP.
Reproduced by permission from *The Oxford Book of Carols*, 1928.

17 Love came down at Christmas

Christina Georgina Rossetti (1830-1894)   Reginald Owen Morris (1886-1948)

TUNE 1: HERMITAGE 67 67

1. Love came down at Christmas,
   Love all lovely, Love divine;
   Love was born at Christmas,
   star and angels gave the sign.

2. Worship we the Godhead,
   Love incarnate, Love divine;
   worship we our Jesus:
   but wherewith for sacred sign?

3. Love shall be our token,
   love be yours and love be mine,
   love to God and all men,
   love for plea and gift and sign.

Christina Georgina Rossetti (1830-1894)   Malcolm Archer (b.1952)

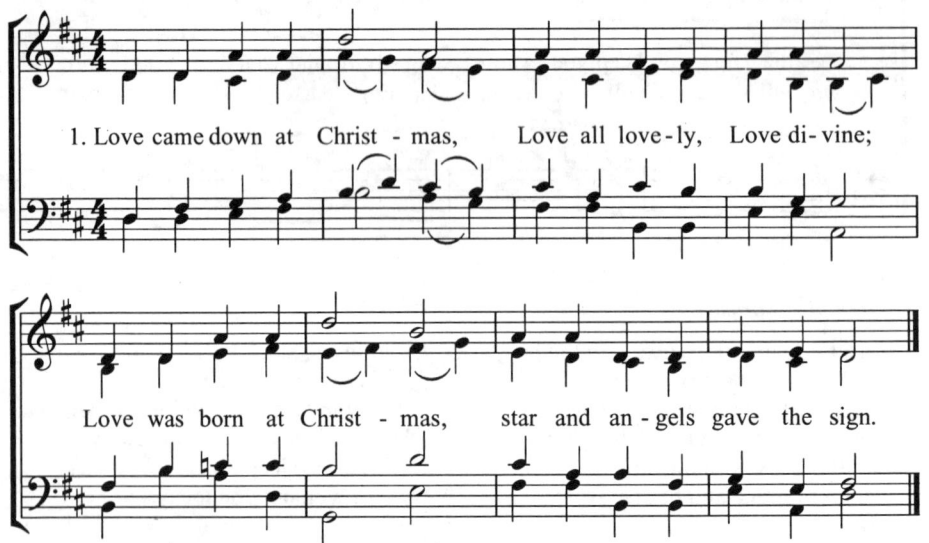

TUNE 2: LOVE CAME DOWN 67 67

1. Love came down at Christmas,
   Love all lovely, Love divine;
   Love was born at Christmas,
   star and angels gave the sign.

Tune 1 © Copyright Oxford University Press, Great Clarendon St., Oxford OX2 6DP. Used by permission.
Tune 2 © Copyright Kevin Mayhew Ltd.

18 Mary had a baby

West Indian Spiritual, alt.

West Indian Spiritual
arr. Colin Mawby

Unison

1. Mary had a baby, yes, Lord, Mary had a baby, yes, my Lord, Mary had a baby, yes, Lord, the people came to Bethlehem to see her son.

2. What did she name him, yes, Lord? *(x3)*
   The people came to Bethlehem to see her son.

3. Mary named him Jesus, yes, Lord, *(x3)*
   the people came to Bethlehem to see her son.

4. Where was he born, yes, Lord? *(x3)*
   The people came to Bethlehem to see her son.

5. Born in a stable, yes, Lord, *(x3)*
   the people came to Bethlehem to see her son.

6. Where did she lay him, yes, Lord? *(x3)*
   The people came to Bethlehem to see her son.

7. Laid him in a manger, yes, Lord, *(x3)*
   the people came to Bethlehem to see her son.

Text and this arrangement © Copyright 1999, 2004 Kevin Mayhew Ltd.

19 O come, all ye faithful

Original Latin attributed to John Francis Wade
trans. Frederick Oakeley (1802-1880)

Attributed to
John Francis Wade (1711-1786)

ADESTE FIDELES Irregular and Refrain

1. O come, all ye faithful, joyful and triumphant, O come ye, O come ye to Bethlehem; come and behold him, born the king of angels:

Refrain
O come,
O come, let us adore him, O come, let us adore him, O

come, let us a-dore him, Christ the Lord.

2. God of God,
   Light of Light,
   lo, he abhors not the Virgin's womb;
   very God, begotten not created:

3. See how the shepherds,
   summoned to his cradle,
   leaving their flocks, draw nigh with lowly fear;
   we too will thither bend our joyful footsteps:

4. Lo, star-led chieftains,
   Magi, Christ adoring,
   offer him incense, gold and myrrh;
   we to the Christ-child bring our hearts' oblations:

5. Child, for us sinners
   poor and in the manger,
   fain we embrace thee, with love and awe;
   who would not love thee, loving us so dearly?

6. Sing, choirs of angels,
   sing in exultation,
   sing, all ye citizens of heav'n above;
   glory to God in the highest:

7. Yea, Lord, we greet thee,
   born this happy morning,
   Jesu, to thee be glory giv'n;
   Word of the Father, now in flesh appearing:

20 Of the Father's love begotten

Corde natus ex parentis by
Aurelius Clemens Prudentius (348-413)
trans. John Mason Neale (1818-1866) alt.

Plainsong melody (13th century)
adapted by Theodoricus Petrus
in *Piae Cantiones* (1582)

CORDE NATUS (DIVINUM MYSTERIUM) 87 87 87 7

1. Of the Father's love begotten, ere the worlds began to be, he is Alpha and Omega, he the source, the ending he, of the things that are, and have been, and that future years shall

see,   e - ver - more   and   e - ver - more.

2. At his word they were created;
   he commanded; it was done:
   heav'n and earth and depths of ocean
   in their threefold order one;
   all that grows beneath the shining
   of the light of moon and sun,
   evermore and evermore.

3. O that birth for ever blessèd,
   when the Virgin, full of grace,
   by the Holy Ghost conceiving,
   bore the Saviour of our race,
   and the babe, the world's Redeemer,
   first revealed his sacred face,
   evermore and evermore.

4. O ye heights of heav'n, adore him;
   angel hosts, his praises sing;
   pow'rs, dominions, bow before him,
   and extol our God and King:
   let no tongue on earth be silent,
   ev'ry voice in concert ring,
   evermore and evermore.

5. This is he whom seers and sages
   sang of old with one accord;
   whom the writings of the prophets
   promised in their faithful word;
   now he shines, the long-expected;
   let our songs declare his worth,
   evermore and evermore.

6. Christ, to thee, with God the Father,
   and, O Holy Ghost, to thee,
   hymn and chant and high thanksgiving,
   and unwearied praises be;
   honour, glory, and dominion,
   and eternal victory,
   evermore and evermore.

21 O little one sweet, O little one mild

Translated from the German
of Samuel Scheidt (1587-1654)
by Percy Dearmer (1867-1936) alt.

Melody from Samuel Scheidt's
Tabulaturbuch (1650)
harm. Martin Shaw (1875-1958)

VERSION 1: O JESULEIN SÜSS 10 9 88 10

1. O little one sweet, O little one mild, thy Father's purpose thou hast fulfilled; thou cam'st from heav'n to dwell below, to share the joys and tears we know. O little one sweet, O little one mild.

2. O little one sweet, O little one mild,
with joy thou hast the whole world filled;
thou camest here from heav'n's domain,
to bring us comfort in our pain,
O little one sweet, O little one mild.

3. O little one sweet, O little one mild,
in thee Love's beauties are all distilled;
then light in us thy love's bright flame,
that we may give thee back the same,
O little one sweet, O little one mild.

Text and Music, Version 1 © Copyright Oxford University Press, Great Clarendon St., Oxford OX2 6DP. Reproduced by permission from *The Oxford Book of Carols*, 1928.

Translated from the German
of Samuel Scheidt (1587-1654)
by Percy Dearmer (1867-1936) alt.

Melody from Samuel Scheidt's
Tabulaturbuch (1650)
harm. Johann Sebastian Bach (1685-1750)

VERSION 2: O JESULEIN SÜSS 10 9 88 10

1. O little one sweet, O little one mild, thy Father's purpose thou hast fulfilled; thou cam'st from heav'n to dwell below, to share the joys and tears we know, O little one sweet, O little one mild.

22 O little town of Bethlehem

Phillips Brooks (1835-1893) alt.

Traditional English melody collected and arr. Ralph Vaughan Williams (1872-1958)

FOREST GREEN DCM

1. O little town of Bethlehem, how still we see thee lie! Above thy deep and dreamless sleep the silent stars go by. Yet in thy dark streets shineth the everlasting light; the hopes and fears of all the years are met in thee tonight.

This arrangement © Copyright Oxford University Press, Great Clarendon St., Oxford OX2 6DP. Reproduced by permission from *The English Hymnal*.

2. O morning stars, together
   proclaim the holy birth,
   and praises sing to God the King,
   and peace to all the earth.
   For Christ is born of Mary;
   and, gathered all above,
   while mortals sleep, the angels keep
   their watch of wond'ring love;

3. How silently, how silently,
   the wondrous gift is giv'n!
   So God imparts to human hearts
   the blessings of his heav'n.
   No ear may hear his coming;
   but in this world of sin,
   where meek souls will receive him, still
   the dear Christ enters in.

4. O holy child of Bethlehem,
   descend to us, we pray;
   cast out our sin, and enter in,
   be born in us today.
   We hear the Christmas angels
   the great glad tidings tell:
   O come to us, abide with us,
   our Lord Emmanuel.

Traditional
Carols

23 Once in royal David's city

Cecil Frances Alexander (1818-1895) alt. Henry John Gauntlett (1805-1876)

IRBY 87 87 77

1. Once in royal David's city stood a lowly cattle shed, where a mother laid her baby in a manger for his bed: Mary was that mother mild, Jesus Christ her little child.

2. He came down to earth from heaven,
who is God and Lord of all,
and his shelter was a stable,
and his cradle was a stall;
with the needy, poor and lowly,
lived on earth our Saviour holy.

3. For he is our childhood's pattern,
day by day like us he grew;
he was little, weak and helpless,
tears and smiles like us he knew;
and he feeleth for our sadness,
and he shareth in our gladness.

4. And our eyes at last shall see him
through his own redeeming love,
for that child so dear and gentle
is our Lord in heav'n above;
and he leads his children on
to the place where he is gone.

This version of text © Copyright 1996 Kevin Mayhew Ltd.

24 On Christmas night all Christians sing

Traditional English carol, alt.

Traditional English melody collected and arr. Ralph Vaughan Williams (1872-1958)

SUSSEX CAROL 88 88 88

1. On Christmas night all Christians sing, to hear the news the angels bring, on Christmas night all Christians sing, to hear the news the angels bring, news of great joy, news of great mirth, news of our merciful King's birth.

Music © Copyright 1919 Stainer and Bell Ltd., P.O. Box 110, Victoria House, 23 Gruneisen Road, Finchley, London N3 1DZ. Used by permission.

2. Then why should we on earth be so sad,
   since our Redeemer made us glad,
   then why should we on earth be so sad,
   since our Redeemer made us glad,
   when from our sin he set us free,
   all for to gain our liberty?

3. When sin departs before his grace,
   then life and health come in its place,
   when sin departs before his grace,
   then life and health come in its place,
   angels and earth with joy may sing,
   all for to see the new-born King.

4. All out of darkness we have light,
   which made the angels sing this night:
   all out of darkness we have light,
   which made the angels sing this night:
   'Glory to God and peace to men,
   now and for evermore. Amen.'

25 See, amid the winter's snow

Edward Caswall (1814-1878)
John Goss (1800-1880)

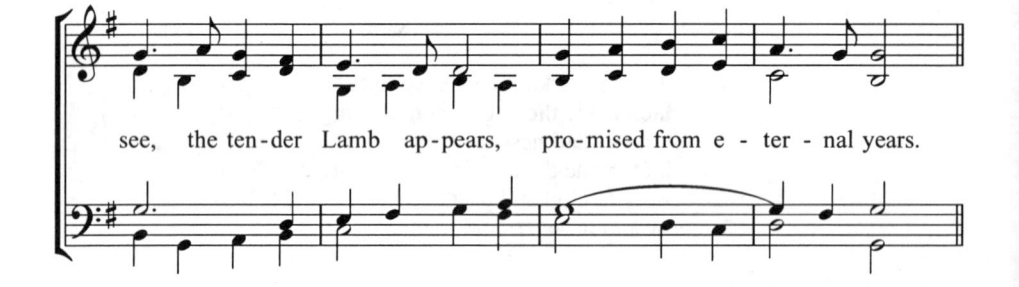

HUMILITY (OXFORD) 77 77 and Refrain

1. See, amid the winter's snow, born for us on earth below, see, the tender Lamb appears, promised from eternal years.

Refrain

Hail, thou ever-blessed morn, hail, redemption's happy dawn! Sing through all Jerusalem, Christ is born in Bethlehem.

2. Lo, within a manger lies
   he who built the starry skies;
   he who, throned in heights sublime,
   sits amid the cherubim.

3. Say, you holy shepherds, say,
   what your joyful news today?
   Wherefore have you left your sheep
   on the lonely mountain steep?

4. 'As we watched at dead of night,
   there appeared a wondrous light;
   angels, singing peace on earth,
   told us of the Saviour's birth.'

5. Sacred infant, all divine,
   what a tender love was thine,
   thus to come from highest bliss,
   down to such a world as this!

Traditional
Carols

26 Silent night

Joseph Mohr (1792-1848)
trans. John Freeman Young (1820-1885)

Franz Grüber (1787-1863)
arr. Colin Hand

STILLE NACHT Irregular

1. Si - lent night, ho - ly night. All is calm, all is bright,
round yon vir - gin mo - ther and child; ho - ly in-fant, so ten-der and mild,
sleep in hea - ven - ly peace, sleep in hea - ven - ly peace.

2. Silent night, holy night.
   Shepherds quake at the sight,
   glories stream from heaven afar,
   heav'nly hosts sing alleluia:
   Christ, the Saviour is born,
   Christ, the Saviour is born.

3. Silent night, holy night.
   Son of God, love's pure light,
   radiant beams from thy holy face,
   with the dawn of redeeming grace:
   Jesus, Lord, at thy birth,
   Jesus, Lord, at thy birth.

This arrangement © Copyright 1994 Kevin Mayhew Ltd.

27 The angel Gabriel from heaven came

Sabine Baring-Gould (1843-1924)
based on *Birjina gaztettobat zegoen*

Traditional Basque melody
arr. Edgar Pettman

GABRIEL'S MESSAGE 10 10 12 7 3

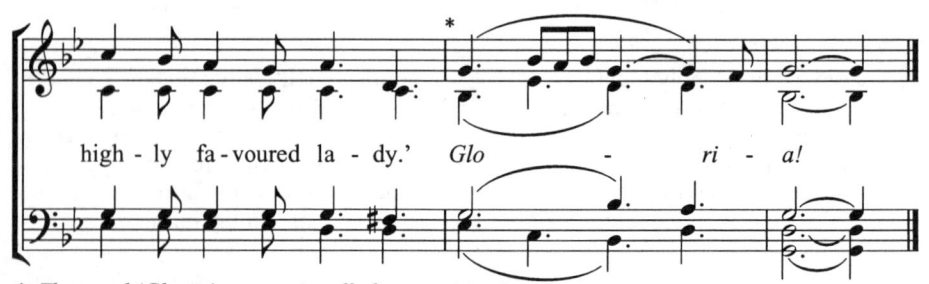

1. The an-gel Ga-bri-el from hea-ven came, his wings as drift-ed snow, his eyes as flame. 'All hail,' said he, 'thou low-ly maid-en, Ma - ry, most high-ly fa-voured la-dy.' Glo - ri - a!

* *The word 'Gloria' may optionally be sung in unison.*

This arrangement © Copyright 1922 H. Freeman & Co./EMI Music Publishing Ltd.
Used by permission of IMP Ltd., Griffin House, 161 Hammersmith Road, London W6 8BS.

2. 'For known a blessèd Mother thou shalt be.
   All generations laud and honour thee.
   Thy Son shall be Emmanuel, by seers foretold,
   most highly favoured lady.' Gloria!

3. Then gentle Mary meekly bowed her head.
   'To me be as it pleaseth God,' she said.
   'My soul shall laud and magnify his holy name.'
   Most highly favoured lady! Gloria!

4. Of her, Emmanuel, the Christ, was born
   in Bethlehem, all on a Christmas morn;
   and Christian folk throughout the world will ever say:
   'Most highly favoured lady.' Gloria!

28 The first Nowell

From William Sandys'
Christmas Carols, Ancient and Modern (1833) alt.

Traditional English melody
arr. John Stainer

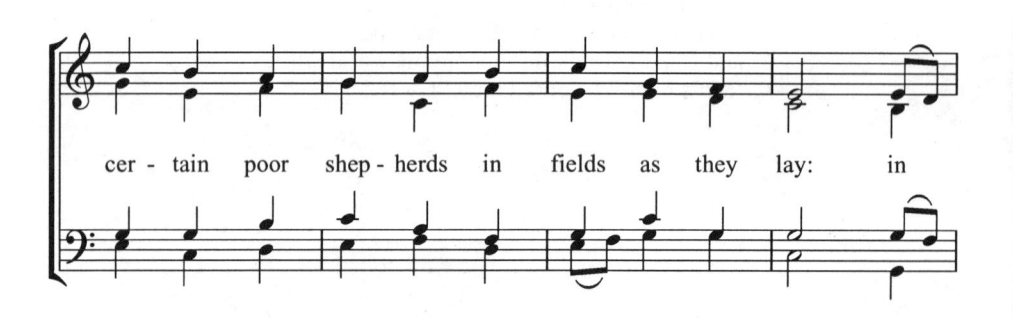

THE FIRST NOWELL Irregular

1. The first Nowell the angel did say was to certain poor shepherds in fields as they lay: in fields where they lay keeping their sheep, on a cold winter's night that was so deep.

Refrain

No-well, No-well, No-well, No-well,
born is the King of Is - ra - el!

2. They lookèd up and saw a star,
   shining in the east, beyond them far,
   and to the earth it gave great light,
   and so it continued both day and night.

3. And by the light of that same star,
   three wise men came from country far;
   to seek for a king was their intent,
   and to follow the star wherever it went.

4. This star drew nigh to the north-west,
   o'er Bethlehem it took its rest,
   and there it did both stop and stay
   right over the place where Jesus lay.

5. Then entered in those wise men three,
   full rev'rently upon their knee,
   and offered there in his presence,
   their gold and myrrh and frankincense.

6. Then let us all with one accord
   sing praises to our heav'nly Lord,
   who with the Father we adore
   and Spirit blest for evermore.

Traditional
Carols

29 The holly and the ivy

Traditional
THE HOLLY AND THE IVY 76 86 (Irregular) and Refrain

English folk carol
arr. Colin Mawby

1. The holly and the ivy, when they are both full grown, of all the trees that are in the wood the holly bears the crown.

Refrain
The rising of the sun and the running of the deer, the playing of the merry or-gan, sweet singing in the choir.

2. The holly bears a blossom,
   white as the lily flower,
   and Mary bore sweet Jesus Christ
   to be our sweet Saviour.

3. The holly bears a berry,
   as red as any blood,
   and Mary bore sweet Jesus Christ
   to do poor sinners good.

4. The holly bears a prickle,
   as sharp as any thorn,
   and Mary bore sweet Jesus Christ
   on Christmas day in the morn.

5. The holly bears a bark,
   as bitter as any gall,
   and Mary bore sweet Jesus Christ
   for to redeem us all.

6. The holly and the ivy,
   when they are both full grown,
   of all the trees that are in the wood
   the holly bears the crown.

This arrangement © Copyright 2004 Kevin Mayhew Ltd.

30 There's a star in the East

American Spiritual

American Spiritual
arr. Malcolm Archer

1. There's a star in the East on Christmas morn, rise up, shepherd, and follow, it will lead to the place where the Saviour's born, rise up, shepherd, and follow. Leave your sheep and leave your lambs, O rise up, shepherd, and follow. Leave your ewes and leave your rams, O

This arrangement © Copyright 1991 Kevin Mayhew Ltd.

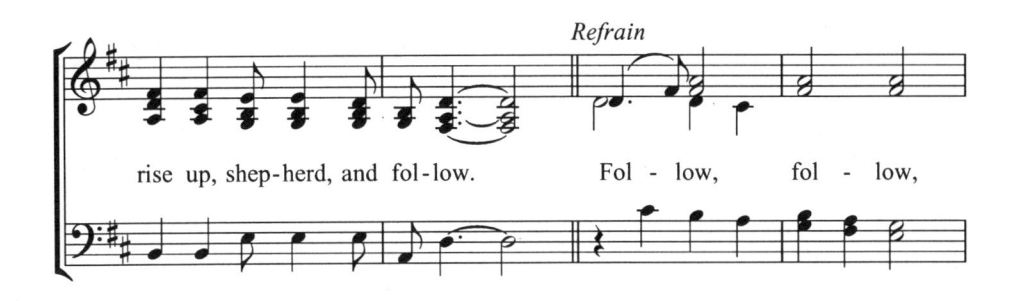

Refrain: rise up, shep-herd, and fol-low. Fol-low, fol-low, rise up, shep-herd, and fol-low. Fol-low the star of Beth-le-hem, rise up, shep-herd, and fol-low.

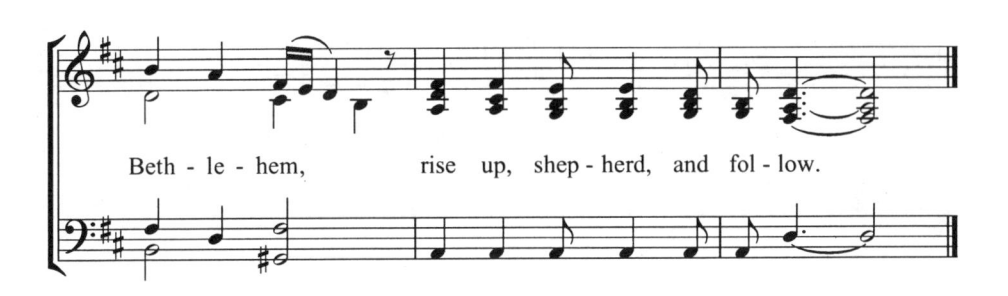

2. If you take good heed of the angel's words,
   rise up, shepherd, and follow,
   you'll forget your flocks, you'll forget your herds,
   rise up, shepherd, and follow.

31 The Virgin Mary had a baby boy

Traditional West Indian

Traditional West Indian
arr. Christopher Tambling

1. The Virgin Mary had a baby boy, the Virgin Mary had a baby boy, the Virgin Mary had a baby boy, and they said that his name was Jesus.

Refrain
He came from the glory, he came from the glorious kingdom. He came from the glory,

This arrangement © Copyright 1994 Kevin Mayhew Ltd.

he came from the glorious kingdom. O yes, believer.

O yes, believer.

He came from the glory, he came from the glorious kingdom.

Vs. 1 & 2 — D.S. — *Last time*

2. The glorious kingdom.

2. The angels sang when the baby was born, *(x3)*
   and proclaimed him the Saviour Jesus.

3. The wise men saw where the baby was born, *(x3)*
   and they saw that his name was Jesus.

Traditional
Carols

32 Unto us a boy is born

Puer nobis nascitur (15th century)
trans. Percy Dearmer (1867-1936) alt.

From *Piae Cantiones* (1582)
arr. Colin Mawby

PUER NOBIS 76 77

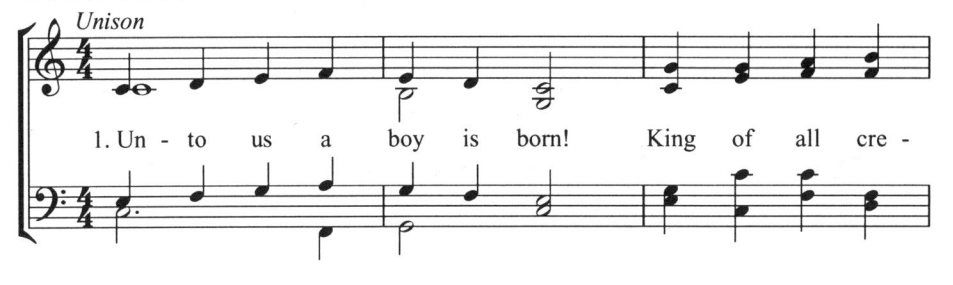

1. Un-to us a boy is born! King of all cre-a-tion; came he to a world for-lorn, the Lord of ev-'ry na-tion, the Lord of ev-'ry na-tion.

2. Cradled in a stall was he,
   watched by cows and asses;
   but the very beasts could see
   that he the world surpasses,
   that he the world surpasses.

3. Then the fearful Herod cried,
   'Pow'r is mine in Jewry!'
   So the blameless children died
   the victims of his fury,
   the victims of his fury.

4. Now may Mary's Son, who came
   long ago to love us,
   lead us all with hearts aflame
   unto the joys above us,
   unto the joys above us.

5. Omega and Alpha he!
   Let the organ thunder,
   while the choir with peals of glee
   shall rend the air asunder,
   shall rend the air asunder.

Text © Copyright Oxford University Press, Great Clarendon St., Oxford OX2 6DP.
Reproduced by permission from *The Oxford Book of Carols*.
This arrangement © Copyright 2004 Kevin Mayhew Ltd.

33 We three kings of Orient are

John Henry Hopkins alt.   John Henry Hopkins (1820-1891)

KINGS OF ORIENT 88 86 and Refrain

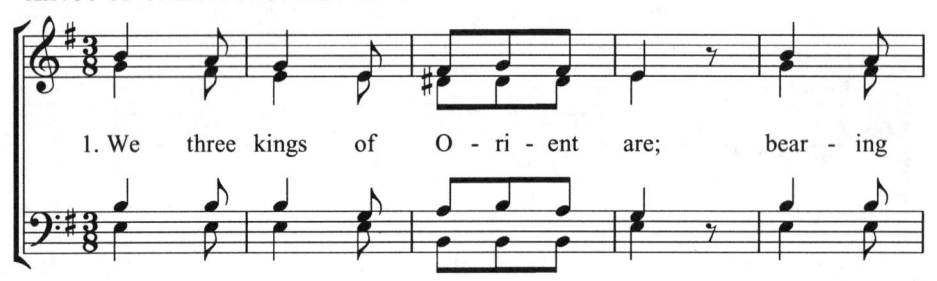

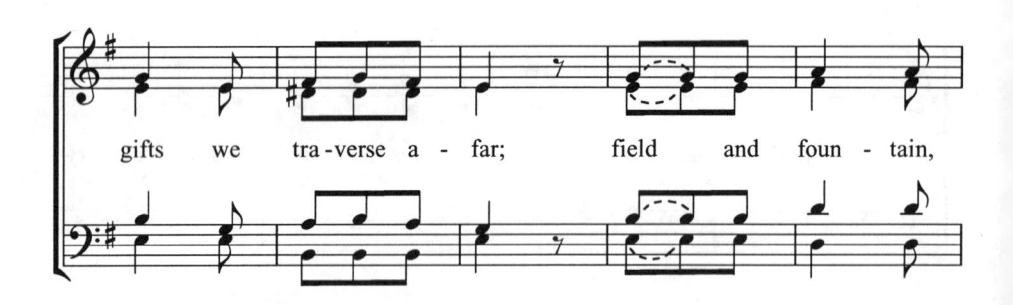

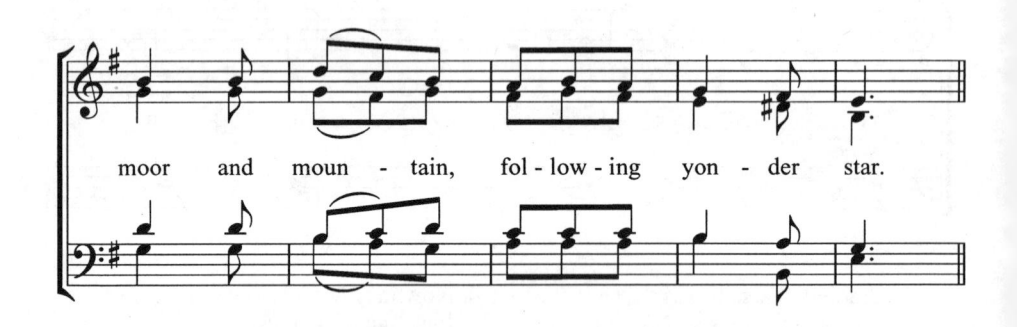

1. We three kings of O-ri-ent are; bear-ing gifts we tra-verse a-far; field and foun-tain, moor and moun-tain, fol-low-ing yon-der star.

Refrain

O star of won-der, star of night,

star with roy-al beau-ty bright, west-ward lead-ing, still pro-ceed-ing, guide us to thy per-fect light.

2. Born a King on Bethlehem plain,
   gold I bring, to crown him again,
   King for ever, ceasing never,
   over us all to reign.

3. Frankincense to offer have I,
   incense owns a Deity nigh,
   prayer and praising, gladly raising,
   worship him, God most high.

4. Myrrh is mine, its bitter perfume
   breathes a life of gathering gloom;
   sorrowing, sighing, bleeding, dying,
   sealed in the stone-cold tomb.

5. Glorious now behold him arise,
   King and God and sacrifice;
   alleluia, alleluia,
   earth to heav'n replies.

34 What child is this

William Chatterton Dix (1837-1898) alt.

Traditional English melody
arr. John Stainer

GREENSLEEVES 87 87 68 67

1. What child is this who, laid to rest, on Mary's lap is sleeping? Whom angels greet with anthems sweet, while shepherds watch are keeping? This, this is Christ the King, whom shepherds guard and angels sing: come, greet the infant Lord, the babe, the Son of Mary!

2. Why lies he in such mean estate,
where ox and ass are feeding?
Good Christians, fear: for sinners here
the silent Word is pleading.
Nails, spear, shall pierce him through,
the cross be borne for me, for you;
hail, hail the Word made flesh,
the babe, the Son of Mary!

3. So bring him incense, gold and myrrh,
come rich and poor, to own him.
The King of kings salvation brings,
let loving hearts enthrone him.
Raise, raise the song on high,
the Virgin sings her lullaby:
joy, joy for Christ is born,
the babe, the Son of Mary!

35 While shepherds watched

Nahum Tate (1652-1715) From Este's *Psalter* (1592)

WINCHESTER OLD CM

1. While shepherds watched their flocks by night, all seated on the ground, the angel of the Lord came down, and glory shone around.

2. 'Fear not,' said he, (for mighty dread
had seized their troubled mind)
'glad tidings of great joy I bring
to you and all mankind.

3. To you in David's town this day
is born of David's line
a Saviour, who is Christ the Lord;
and this shall be the sign:

4. The heav'nly babe you there shall find
to human view displayed,
all meanly wrapped in swathing bands,
and in a manger laid.'

5. Thus spake the seraph, and forthwith
appeared a shining throng
of angels praising God, who thus
addressed their joyful song:

6. 'All glory be to God on high,
and on the earth be peace,
goodwill henceforth from heav'n to all
begin and never cease.'

Also available

THE ULTIMATE CAROL BOOK
101 settings for choirs

1 84417 244 9
M57024 334 1
1450319

One of the most comprehensive carol books around, features 101 of the most popular carols for SATB choirs.

- Traditional carols from across the centuries
- Classic arrangements by Charles Wood, John Stainer
- Modern arrangements of old favourite carols
- New carols by Malcolm Archer, Sarah Watts and others
- Many carols with descants included
- Accompaniments where appropriate